More Praise for *Flatlands*

Written in the key of Willa Cather and in kinship with the spare and located writing practice of Lorine Niedecker, Ruth Williams' *Flatlands* could very well be a continuation of the Prairie Trilogy. A subtle defiance circulates through these poems—a book of mouths—whose investments include the erotics of place, gender expectations, insecurity, and boredom—the "radical blah" that fills in and out so much of a life. Williams works through what it means to be from and in a place, understanding we are shaped by land and language. In an era of platitudes, I admire the reluctance in these poems, balanced by awe that our bodies may be our best souvenirs—"I don't mean to make more of it/ than I should.// We are all envelopes/ of loose teeth." Reading Williams' poems, I feel a little less weary about being a packet of debris, about being, in general.
—**Kristi Maxwell, author of** *That Our Eyes Be Rigged*

In *Flatlands*, Ruth Williams turns her surroundings into well-crafted poems that deeply explore the physical and metaphorical landscape. We glimpse youth growing into maturity through a lens of desire and the elusive nature of love. Williams' poems are filled with imagery, making inventive use of repetition ("Radical Blah" and "Sister" poems), syntax ("Surviving on Equations"), surprising, delicious sounds ("His Gorgette"), and more. Her poems wisely lead us up to the edge, to the sense that there's more beneath what is said. A fine collection.
—**Twyla M. Hansen, Nebraska State Poet, author of** *Rock • Tree • Bird*

Flatlands
Ruth Williams

Black
Lawrence
Press

 Black Lawrence Press

www.blacklawrence.com

Executive Editor: Diane Goettel
Book and Cover Design: Amy Freels
Cover Art: "untitled" by Oleg Oprisco

Copyright © 2018 Ruth Williams
ISBN: 978-1-62557-989-8

All rights reserved. Except for brief quotations in critical articles or reviews, no part of this book may be reproduced in any manner without prior written permission from the publisher: editors@blacklawrencepress.com

Published 2018 by Black Lawrence Press.
Printed in the United States.

for Joe

Contents

I.

Humboldt Fault	3
Picking Strawberries	5
Ignition	6
Grassland Antelope	7
One-Room Schoolhouse	8
Radical Blah	9
Physiography	10
Sisters, We Must Claim Our Origins	11
How We Came to the Hill	12
Lover's Leap Butte	13
Radial Plain	14

II.

Each Touch Leaves an Imprint	19
His Gorgette	21
Crisp Knot	22
Lengthy Silences	23
Roost Her	24
Goldenrod	25
Delicate	26
Unnaturally Attracted to Hills	28
Canyon	29
Running Froth	30
Radical Blah	31
Parting Shots	32
Thug Weather	33

Sisters, We Must Harden Our Own Honey	34
Last Line, Dropped	35
Unstabled	36
Felt Bigger Driving on Empty	37
Light Posts	38

III.

Dugout	41
Side Effect of Flat Land	42
Surviving On Equations	44
Plain Winter	45
Bitterroot	46
Sisters, We Must Receive Her Gift	48
Import	49
Cutting Dry Hair	50
Radical Blah	51
Lord Knows	52
The Deer	53
Shadow Play	54
Dumbfounded	56
Premonition	58
Solstice	59
Sounds Like Animals at Night	60
Jackalope	61
An Entrepreneurial Mindset	62
Notes	63
Acknowledgments	64

We agreed that no one who had not grown up in a little prairie town could know anything about it. It was a kind of freemasonry, we said.
—Willa Cather, *My Ántonia*

I.

Humboldt Fault

As children
we pirouetted, tipsy
ballerinas tripping
through wet grass.

The great fault beneath:
gap like an inverted lens
hidden beneath
square-shoulder fields,

a fact we forgot
by the end of
grade school.

Nebraska
hypnotizes eyes
with slow lines: straight
highway blurring
into horizon.

Lulled in the strand
of our history, we were like
the Platte River,
its mud sluice easy to follow
out through the plains.

The ready-made disaster
subtle as a shift in the wind:
unreadable, all around us.

Picking Strawberries

One in the bucket,
one in my mouth. I ate them
with dirt, ate
until my throat was raked.

My mother told me I inherited a taste
for acid, a stinging champagne.

The tender skin of my mouth
dotted with red pulp, tiny seeds
burrowed between teeth. A little hardness
to occupy the tongue.

I would eat more as we left for home.
I would eat as we washed them at the sink,
hulled their stems.

Those nights, I dreamt
I gulped, swallowing
into a red hangover.

I woke. My mouth open and opening.
I'd inherited a taste for air.

Ignition

Fireworks rushed their explosions, stumbling
flung swatches of drunken color. The sky blurred,
pink, yellow, red—a whirling slip of lights.

We thought, this must be what adults meant by intense:
the red flare, a tongue reaching out,
lapping from the clustered fuse.

The hillside slowly bent under the sky's flame. Scorched
paper sifted warm over our faces, heads. Tapping
our shoulders, our parents turned us away.

We tried to shake their grasp, look back.
In the firelight, ash floated like loose hairs;
pricking our cheeks in the cooling air.

Riding home, even as we curled
in the pocket of our parents' stillness, we kept
the night's heat in our fists, ready to knock.

Grassland Antelope

He strikes the pose
of an inquisitive visitor.

Steady legs, craned head.
A flock of alert lines, still angles.

On the plain, a geometric pattern replicated
is a row. Divine the organizing principle.

Note: At times, beauty comes complete
with a roll-back lid.

One-Room Schoolhouse

We dressed
as pioneers: long dresses,
bonnets,
a pocket slate.

Sketching ships
across the waves of grass,
the lesson chalked
our hands.

Mimicking geography
we lanced the morning,
letting sunset seep
across the plains.

The windows
reflected our own faces
back to us,
such looks of desire,

we wanted to reap
whatever it was
the plain dresses
could sow in us.

Radical Blah

In every plains town,
all night trains whistle
a dark bell sound.

On TV, a pet weasel emerges
from between the bed and wall
again and again, body
like a little brown finger,
beckoning.

Outside, the leaves wave back.
The early autumn is
a basket to weave one's hair into.
I ask for mine to be pulled.

Open the nostrils, tip the head
and the eyes bulge
from their sockets.

Boredom becomes
a bitter pleasure.
Over the landscape, then,
a cold red fit.

Physiography

Flatlands,
the pat of a hand
on your head. A good girl,
a slicing edge. Like a scythe
through grass you learn to love
the sound of cutting hair. An ingrained
lust for a portion reduced. You flat
your body like a white wafer
and you mean it to be religious.
Like a frontier church,
you give yourself up to horizon,
so being put in your place
is like a cross on your flat back.

Sisters, We Must Claim Our Origins

Grandma reads the horoscopes
so our eyes go wide.

There's a white dog like mist
chained to the back of the garage—
its bark searching the fog.

The pond is stocked
with easy-to-catch fish who eat
table scraps, turn marble eyes up
through the muck.

Grandma says there's nothing like the taste
of something you've grown yourself. Her fingers
and ours glisten with frying oil, salt.

In the old days, the men of the family
kept stills, carried guns. Now, we drink moonshine
in the parking lot at the reunion.

My sister's hands shake,
but the taste is of fruit,
low register of heat.

We're not children, but it's easy
to believe in magic. So much of our wildness
cannot be predicted, though the rust on us
surely is a lesson to be read.

How We Came to the Hill

In that time, we walked
with silver toes:
a chorus of tinkly chimes.

We were girls, a multiphonic
band of gong—all echo

and a thrump: the ax slap
of metronomic heartbeats
ticking in the deep well of hips.

Though we allowed ourselves
to be led to the field, willingly,
we were heart skip, hiccup and up—

that hill, its one stop, its end,
our reckoning—deep
and purple.

Lover's Leap Butte

Early on, I learned to love
the feel of fingers curled
in a giant rug, some bison fur,
horned head reduced
to a hump.

That beast was quiet,
but later, when I had my first kiss,
I knew the sound of dogs
was what I could expect.

They howled like tongues
whipping the grass. He and I,
biting each other
to keep warm.

I'd grow up, kicking rocks
softly, then pushing
the larger ones over the edge. As if
to test what reaction
the action of falling is.

Radial Plain

> *As she lay with her eyes closed, she had again, more vividly than for many years, the old illusion of her girlhood, of being lifted and carried lightly by someone very strong [...] She knew at last for whom it was she had waited, and where he would carry her.*
> —Willa Cather, *O Pioneers!*

In my 13th year, hanging
the laundry, the white sheets
were like blowsy dresses
and my heartache

was a new
nostalgia, the plains
the leavening,

grasses a long cry,
the hair of my later years
growing before me.

How I spent that summer
like Cather, wanting
the strong arms

of another coming
round me, knowing
that this too was a foretaste

of what it meant to be flattened,
to love like the dirt,
hard, packed,

how fertile then
not to know what
I would become.

II.

Each Touch Leaves an Imprint

His knife plinks the salmon's ribs.
Organs spread, a girl's coral dress
come undone.

Overhead, gulls wing
against the sky, angled shapes
that collapse as they drop.

He has a sure grip. The blood sticks
in a loam under his nails. For him,
love and the hesitation it breeds
are a long way off.

He tells me to put my hands in the body;
the birds' beaks flash orange.
He does not yet know
how it feels to be taken, held this way.

My fingers slip through the silk of entrails,
blind tips that nose the belly. Here,
I feel the bowl and suck of current,
there the thrust toward air.

I fling the guts, cast
as he's shown me. The birds
circle, swoop.

He laughs as they dip
and rise, empty-mouthed.
The current's shifted;
a girl's long neck, turned.

His Gorgette

Block throat, cock-wide canker. I am
flanged to spine you, wound-wanker. Hang on

to another name for this. Love
to make you skin-gorged, ganked to my plank.

What plink? What marble
shims me? You must be shank-in.

Portion full, I am fattened. In my backyard,
the hipped slank gleans. Gathering

your finger, the fence spreads
its puffer quills.

Crisp Knot

Can't forget Gulliver:
hair stretched above head,
hands at his sides. All over him,
small people crawl, tying knots.

The rope, a peaceful latticework
snugs him. His fattest parts
fill the holes.

In a bodywork maze
one cannot be too sure
of direction.

Cardinal feathers
make a ghostly outline
around the ordinal hands.

Who can chart
the movement of breath? No math
makes sense to tight lungs.

The knot is a pleasure. The body tethered
in order to be unraveled
by many threads.

Lengthy Silences

Once, cars were
smooth-riding greyhounds
ambling across the pavement.

Roads curved to appear, then disappear
like the erotic tease of a man
wearing a necklace
just below his shirt.

At his collar,
the bones lace, delicate,
well-oiled.

Lately, I have not been moved
to seethe or suckle
any one piece of skin, but lo,
I have longed for
the lengthened road.

Discovering the wide, old
boulevards of the city. Driving until
my body's lost or scattered,
a nostalgic sunset fragmenting sight.

Roost Her

Yes, I remember the rooster's red
coxcomb. It seemed so genital,
exposed to the elements. This too
was masculinity, it seemed.

At the time, my family collected feathers
from wild birds as we had no farm.
We made dioramas and I always used
the smallest, most white
for my boy's hair.

Now, I see your beard grow
from the black tip out to the white stroke
and my hands seek out
some red comb to drag
through, through.

Goldenrod

The golden curve
of a tightened fist unfurls
a little.

So you can
take the whole plant
in your hand.

Another time
suggests itself; girls
rubbing yellow dandelions
on their skin—

some game
of permanence, marriage. But
the count's off.

It's the wrong flower. Seems
you've got the wrong
categorization of the world.

Delicate

Out West, antelope nibbled the grass,
petite ballerinas bowed to a bar.
Their origami limbs held
the poise of tight creases,
a row of knees unsprung.

When you pulled the wheel toward them
the car swerved and you laughed,
not cruelly, but I was happy

when they moved away.
A turn of heads, simultaneous;
a full-hand slap, a snap—

like beige coats
gaining momentum, their bodies
a blare of stoppered yells
set careening.

What did you want from them?
The feel of blood in slender veins,
a flare of pulses that would quicken
under your palm?

I wanted to unravel
like a streamer tethered
to their legs, fold my limbs
in a graceful arch

like these animals
who drape themselves
over gravity

to lure it
into letting them bend
far away from us.

Unnaturally Attracted to Hills

On the news, I heard some kids were killed
hill jumping.

The car went off the road,
hit a concrete encasement.

When I was young,
my father drove these hills fast

to make our stomachs
drop away. Cut off

the blood to our heads. Now,
entertaining myself with myself,

I have trouble feeling my own body.
There is a spring archness

to everything. A bending, like a wick
burned down into itself.

What calls out
from the asphalt's shimmer?

The stand of trees, a thrill. The pavement,
a dog lunging. In white fear light,

there's a shrill pleasure in
the banality of the bite.

Canyon

Looks like purple plums
at the bottom of the Grand Canyon.
That's why the sky settled down into it.

Drawn by dusky skin, digging in
to the red parts, some pulp. Who
wouldn't want to split it?

As the donkeys are led, carefully,
so their ankles won't break,
so too have I been

harnessed by your rock
hoof slipping. Drawn,
willingly,

the bowl of fruit I carried on my head,
somehow gone when I got
to the bottom of it.

Running Froth

The paper lanterns are boats,
glancing off the shine of waves, riding edges
as if they're your body. Or this
is what I'm thinking, aflame,
your parchment skin
an imposition on the world.
I do not know if this is what is meant by
you'll know it when you see it, but
iridescence seems enough
to chart, wicking out patterns
in the turnstiles of water. That's the obsession,
drawing finger-path mazes,
then walking through as if a god
balancing on your wave's difficult cape.
I'm losing parts of the metaphor,
but here is the lantern, fire
slowly disheartening itself across paper,
and your face, the dissipating burn.

Radical Blah

Next door,
a child's bronchial cough
like the sound of something
being flattened, over
and over.

In the shower,
I touch my breasts
fingers moving in slow circles.
It is a female movement
that bores me.

The torsion of the horizon here
full of brown buildings
makes all noise echo.
No one can tell
what is what.

But always the chop, chop
of hospital helicopters overhead, lifting
the emergency away.

Parting Shots

The weather is silty, but the fresh rain fills
the trash barrels, nonetheless.

Someone come along
and say it glistens, yes? So natural,

it's uncanny, isn't it? The way
Canadian geese mate for life

and swim, tenderly honking
through the water.

We would do well to web our feet,
give ourselves feathers, lick

what comes from a spent seed.
Hooved and curved,

our beaks pierce
the heart,

just another
grasping thing.

Thug Weather

Here, the buildings
wait alone, shadows witch tall

while the white squirrel poses
as if it were an omen. All action happens

in the mind. All meaning
in archival accrual.

Everyone here wishes for curled toes, multiple orgasms.
New, more environmental cars.

Mostly, they long to be in Chicago.
Big, brotherly brute of a city. Sulfur smelling pig.

I lived in your binds too long.

Now, untwinned in this city of doubles,
I'm unslick with my hoarding hips.

Wool hats pile at my feet in a muted yarn.
Where are my many screaming heads?

It turns out: I am only a mouth
inside a mouth inside a mouth.

Sisters, We Must Harden Our Own Honey

In French, a verb can be forced into the active form
with the application of -*ant*. So outside, snow falls,
inflamed cells in need of cooling—*ant, ant*.

No more of grandfather's honey to dapple, to glen.
Soured, our aunt's cancered guts strain her stitched stomach.
A long tube of oxygen floats through the room.

Somewhere warmer a man charms a snake, makes it sit up,
beg for air. To lift our aunt from the toilet, my grandmother
wedges herself tight in a small wooden chair.

Gathering the dappled intestine
like a beehive juicy with snakes, we harden,
preserve a mordant honey.

But I want to be on fire in the bees' glen. Then,
the firemen would be taken with me. Flumed with emergency
in the apple core time of winter.

Decay, that red elbow of pain indwelling:
an inheritance, a natural correspondence.
Some unholy *ant* inside us.

Last Line, Dropped

The watermark on the desk is a finger trace
of some broader magic.

Black fronds whipping about the head
as if one is a piece of meat.

I feel light, crisp,
my lawn aerated with holes.

Earlier, I dipped into an article
on trephination

and felt more roomy. My dark
longings, a set of bangs

shaggy for trimming. I have
grown into extra weight,

found some abject comfort there,
my shadow leaving greater,

then greater marks.

Unstabled

There comes a dusty smell,
the closed-off room

giving itself earth. A tidy mien
is nothing to this plentitude

of brown, then bug rot, then dirt.
What did your mother say would clean

a dirty mouth? A knotted rag,
a bitter citrus?

Those were tools
we fancied ourselves using,

but we were adults, we chose instead
to seize the worn, dark wood

between our teeth. A depressor,
no harmony there, just blasted tongues.

Felt Bigger Driving on Empty

The half-built, abandoned hotel looses
shadow puppet selves,
other versions of travel. Days
when we would drive everywhere, pay
to stay in nice places. The kind
that have free cable, all the ice you need
and a seal on the toilet to tell you
what was clean before you arrived.
Such luxury then, in leaving traces. How
happy we were, using it up. Now,
this place is sunk in on itself,
electric cords ripped
like gizzards from the walls. Still,
you can't leave a lifeless thing
more lifeless. Nothing cleaner than
having never fully been.

Light Posts

60-degree weather,
mid-January, porch door
open, so I'm swimming
 in the slow wish, wish
of traffic. An old song
from before I was born,
playing in the other room.
A woman's voice
beautifully muffled.
Is a trapped thing
more alluring caught
in the wrong season?
I move my hands,
cover the light to see
what emerges
when it springs back.
Over the phone,
the wind blows
in another part of the country
and I hear it translated
into something—I can't tell—
is it freeing itself
from here
or there?

III.

Dugout

The air is cool in a sod house. Snakes
curl in the corners like spades
without any earth to dig.

In the old days, they'd let the cow graze
on the roof. Some slow, slipping steps
above the bed.

A fine sifting of dirt covers
the mouth like snakeskin. The drying
corn rustling like limbs.

Over the prairie, you can't
see what was. Dust to dust,
as they say,

those houses now,
just comfortable hollows
in the earth.

Side Effect of Flat Land

In my hometown, I go out
on a plains level night
to seek exquisiteness,
a shred of excess. To ferret out
the hair-raising pain of a rotting tooth,
brush electric
against the sinkhole past.

At the bar I see a man
I knew seven years ago.
His eyes oil-slick
with their back draft of black.

On him, the static of my youth.
All that cling and cower,
my old nerves jangling.

I hinge, a fan
of scattered desire. Wax
salvific: a halo
on the yellowing past.

My eyes rim horizon's edge
for the stomach-lurch of gravity.
That titillating reach.

Through the window,
the echo of flat land thuds—
words come. Words go.

No hills in the way.

Surviving On Equations

The day is the longest thread,
continuing out and out and out.

Mirage: a piece of light tricks
the floor to spark. The shard
of shattered glass.

Shell: a sweater with a button off,
the two sides
in a lopsided embrace.

The night is the longest bowl,
continuing down and down and down.

Nightshade: something escapes in sleep,
the huff of a dream scrapes
along the pillow.

Halo: fantasize the body
to supple, a strand
that sings under fingers.

Even so, the terrible gape
of the tongue wagging in air:

a blind pig snuffling
the taut skin
of a ripe fruit.

Plain Winter

The winter lengthens. The blank horizon is a way
of being more profound than snow. Inside it, a lantern
swatch of yellow curling over a buried leg.

In pioneer days, they'd tie frozen
bodies to the fencepost. The twine a way of
waiting for spring.

Bitterroot

On me: the stuffed face
of adolescent sweat,
puffed curve
of a swelling jaw.

Medusa smile,
short of pained: peek
of two front teeth, little white hats
dangle on a faded strip
of coral lips.

Inside my mouth's sheen, a fish flops.
Scales stick to my tongue
in iridescent ribbons. I suck
on muscle: the tensile
piece of it, the slopping
mass of it.

Everywhere I go,
people chuckle,
shift thin strips of air
through mouths. Half-laughs
dribble out.

They say, life
is a series
of successes.

You know, one
after the other.

Sisters, We Must Receive Her Gift

On the bed, my aunt's quilt.
All the state birds
painted square-by-square, but badly,
colors smeared as if their wings
were still flexing.

Years ago, the sparrow I caught
in the mesh net was like a soft seed. Entrapped,
I could run my hands
round its body.

No, not sleek, the bones were
unfeminine, the wings dusty. Still,
the delicate heart fluttering underneath
felt sensitive. I kept it there
longer than I needed.

Now that my aunt's gone,
I sleep in her state. Palms translating
the movement of paint
into places.

I've learned migrations
are inherited patterns. A woman
walks into them,
but the bird sets off
on its own gifted trajectory.

Import

On TV, the fattest man in the world
says his body was the result of
childhood issues.

It's a practiced explanation
I know.

Significantly, he notes,
he began losing weight
when his mother died.

His arms
hang with wings
the pretty doctor
says she'll
clip.

I don't mean to make more of it
than I should.

We are all envelopes
of loose teeth.

Cutting Dry Hair

The light from the moon gets tangled,
falls on the wrong thing: a winter fly buzzing
across the floor like a tapping shoe.

Premature visitor. The temperature falls
throughout the day, a big gust at the door,
a leak down the hall. Whose ghost?

A séance requires sticky fingers,
and no one believes in that kind of magic.
Your own insincere legs lift the table.

I have written three clichés about my body
and stood among them. Female,
bored. Already tucked into bed.

Radical Blah

Parking lot black,
one lone man
collects the same cart
over and over.

Or it only appears
the same.

The world is on a reel
and no one's skirt is up,
but in winter
everyone hustles.

That's enough movement
to believe in
spiritual strings.

I grew up with a toy box
and know how to
offer containment
its outlet.

The lid
screwed up,
the wheels rolling away.

Lord Knows

Kidding aside, the curb felt wonderful,
its densities that I could keep for my own.

That was the cement of "alone,"
then something beyond it.

You think: people's mouths move silently
in a room full of ghosts.

So I wanted to hold, not my old friends,
but the tender roots of a new tree.

To feel whatever melody could
skip. To trace whatever that meant.

We are adults and should know,
but I cannot stop counting the hills

up to my childhood home.
The driveways all laid out like dimes, heads up.

The Deer

They lived among us quietly,
in the slim stand of trees.

We thought them, then, almost magical,
not realizing they were
simple, doglike creatures.

Often, there was a fluttering
in our peripheral vision. While our
eyes were looking elsewhere

we'd feel their movement, hook
onto the hoof of one, the white tail
of another

and be moving ourselves
as if that was nature's call—
to drag us from the sidewalk

into some other
darker brush.

Shadow Play

The fox on the wall steps
foot light, graceful.
Tail high, it turns into

a rabbit's ear,
twitching end
a rounded nub,

a camel's hump
lumbering forward,
dry-mouthed,

in search of water,
an elephant's
swinging head

rears up to become a bear,
big-shouldered,
mouth open

to the split tail
of a fish, flickering
in deep shadow,

a suggestion of
movement, birds hiding
in the dark,

wings folded,
the woman waits
to present

herself,
a new shape
for the taking.

Dumbfounded

No need for driving rain
to wash you. I prefer messes,
I consoled myself.

There wasn't anything
true about that.

I only wanted to write
like a shirt turned inside out, tags
gone cryptic upside down.

To create a vague sense
of discomfort.
A rock in the shoe, a piece of floss
stuck between teeth.

Like driving around
the city of your birth
but out where
all the new shops went in.

A set of cul-de-sacs
to destroy you.

Like a tonic,
a talisman, you repeat:
keep your palm
on the left-hand side.

No matter the maze, that's how
you'll find your way out.

Premonition

There is a shuffling in the eaves, spring,
some animals reproducing. You are

a breathing terrarium, but
the scattered leaves

tell something else. Your eyes burn
in an afterimage of fall.

Can you derive the face of God
from your reflection?

The day like a TV playing
in the back room, all echo voice.

Yet, something warm
approaching from far off.

After all, who can cup your skin
as tightly as you can?

Solstice

Weather like
warm wallpaper,
smack of a slick back
onto chest, arms,
enveloping the body
until it blends
into summer's pattern:
light, not light. So
one could imagine
glossy tethers in our dark hair—no
crown of flowers,
something more
fierce, light hooked
to position heads. Uncanny
how the white of it makes
everything both
more defined
and more painful,
so we find
our eyes reined in,
viewing things askance,
never fully knowing
what faces us, yet
feeling assured
by the shadows
something is there.

Sounds Like Animals at Night

A luster luxe, the halo
from the farm's electric light.
Oh, to live in the handmade,
hoary, delicate and yet,
so far outside.

Is it possible
you could ask yourself
something, then
answer

as if you too
were the echo
of the highway
off the side
of the barn?

A rustic scene
always rumbles,
reads its—

some might want to say
palm, but
I know better. I say
mouth.

Jackalope

The prairie
demands décollage.

In strips,
tear the grass away

to a light hare. The horns,
a shadow branch

that oscillates
in a mythic drowse.

The hair
around each bone

moves lightly
as if bewitching.

Touch it,
and now you're outlined,

torn into
shape. Oh, yes—

you're being
found.

An Entrepreneurial Mindset

From work, the road feels doubly long.
Or reversed, the houses now,
at night, unfamiliar presences
tentatively taking shape. Like deer
nosing from the woods,
the yellow blinks of windows bump,
bump, bump to black.
On the radio, a woman announces
the local blood supply is blinking out.
It's been too cold. It's not
that we're less generous. We've always
wanted to give. All along,
you've been repeating the same
hesitant movements,
just slower. It's the same
old road, you're just newer,
you're new.

Notes

"Humboldt Fault": This is a series of fault zones that extend from the southeast corner of Nebraska into Kansas.

"Lover's Leap Butte": Located on the grounds of Fort Robinson State Park in the "panhandle" region of Nebraska, this 4,390 foot summit is the highest in the state. According to legend, a pair of young lovers from warring Native American tribes were forbidden to be together. Rather than live without each other, they jumped to their deaths from the ridge. Given that such a tale is told about other summits in the U.S. similarly called "Lover's Leap," it is unlikely that this story is true.

"Radial Plain": In Willa Cather's novel *O Pioneers!,* the main character, Alexandra Bergson, has a series of reoccurring dreams in which she is carried across the plains in the arms of a male figure she calls the "mightiest of lovers."

"Goldenrod": The goldenrod is the state flower of Nebraska. It is commonly found in open grassland areas. The game referenced in this poem is the childhood practice of rubbing dandelions on skin until they leave a yellow mark. In one version of the game, the bigger the yellow mark, the more you were said to be "boy crazy."

Acknowledgments

"Sisters, We Must Claim Our Origins" and "Sisters, We Must Receive Her Gift," *Pembroke Magazine*, No. 49, Spring 2017.

"Lover's Leap Butte" and "Radial Plain," *Zone 3*, Vol. 31, No. 2, Fall 2016.

"Solstice" and "Sisters, We Must Harden Our Own Honey," *Potomac Review*, Issue 58, Spring 2016.

"An Entrepreneurial Mindset," *Cimarron Review*, Issue 193, Fall 2015.

"Light Posts" and "Lengthy Silences," *Arroyo Review*, Issue 7, Spring 2015.

"Surviving on Equations," *Cider Press Review*, Vol. 17, Issue 1. Jan. 2015.

"Delicate," *Cumberland River Review*, Issue 3.2, Spring 2014.

"Picking Strawberries" and "Plain Winter," *The Untidy Season: An Anthology of Nebraska Women Poets*, Backwaters Press, September 2013.

"His Gorgette," *Alice Blue Review*, Issue 13. February 2011.

"Thug Weather," *Barn Owl Review*, No. 3. Spring 2010.

"Each Touch Leaves an Imprint," *42 Opus*, Vol. 8, No. 3. 28 Sept. 2008.

"Ignition," *Hubbub*, Vol. 23. Spring 2007.

"Humboldt Fault," *Lake Effect*, Vol. 10. Spring 2006.

Thank you to the editors of the journals listed above for publishing my work and to Diane Goettel and the team at Black Lawrence Press for bringing this book into the world.

Many thanks also to those who have thoughtfully read my poems and provided me with essential feedback on the journey toward this book, including my poetry teachers at Eastern Washington University and the University of Cincinnati. A special thanks Nance Van Winckel and Don Bogen whose mentorship has been invaluable to my growth as a poet and teacher of creative writing. Thank you also to the many friends who have read and commented on my work along the way, including Matt McBride, Lisa Ampleman, Kristi Maxwell, Elizabeth Harmon, Kim Lambright, Brian Clifton, and Andrew Reeves. I am also grateful to Barbara Varanka for the Patterns of Art group whose prompts spurred a few of these poems into life.

A thank you also goes to my parents and sisters for showing me "the good life" in Nebraska, inspiring several of the poems here. I am also indebted to Joy Callahan, who suggested way back in 9th grade that I should write a poem, setting me off down the path to this point.

And, finally, thank you to Joe DeLong, who suggested I pull my old and new work together, sparking this book into creation. You're the "ou-u" to my "Caribou."

Photo: Kira Whitney

Ruth Williams is the author of *Conveyance* (Dancing Girl Press, 2012). Her poetry has appeared in *Michigan Quarterly Review*, *jubilat*, *Pleiades* and *Third Coast* among others. She has also published creative nonfiction in *DIAGRAM* and *Crab Orchard Review* as well as scholarly work on women's writing and feminism in *Tulsa Studies in Women's Literature*, *The Journal of Popular Culture*, and *College Literature*. Currently, Ruth lives in Kansas City where she is an Assistant Professor of English at William Jewell College and an editor for *Bear Review*.